Eavesdrop Soup

Matt Cook

Manic D Press
San Francisco

A slightly different version of "The Matches in Our Matchbook" originally appeared in *Anthills*.

Library of Congress Cataloging-in-Publication Data

Cook, Matt, 1969-
  Eavesdrop soup / Matt Cook.
    p. cm.
  ISBN 1-933149-00-0 (pbk. : alk. paper)
  1. Middle West—Poetry. 2. Blue collar workers—Poetry. I. Title.
  PS3603.O574E228 2005
  811'.6—dc22

                                                    2005006149

for Meredith

CONTENTS

"If here ain't the Harrisburg Mail at last, and dreadful bright and smart to look at too," cried an elderly gentleman in some excitement, "darn my mother."

I don't know what the sensation of being darned may be, or whether a man's mother has a keener relish or disrelish of the process than anybody else; but if the endurance of this mysterious ceremony by the old lady in question had depended on the accuracy of her son's vision in respect to the abstract brightness and smartness of the Harrisburg Mail, she would certainly have undergone its infliction.

— Charles Dickens, American Notes (1842)

Part One

Songbirds

I'm half paying attention to a poet talking about dying.
It's a serious matter, but I'm confident he's handling it all wrong.
The possible variations that can bring about
Satisfying zucchini bread are finite.
Your uncle smells roughly the same as your father;
You always want the worst fork in the best restaurant.
I'm worried that the spider on my ceiling
Is part of a poem you've already heard before.
The worthless songbirds are up in the trees again—
I can't believe that they still call Bulgaria *Bulgaria*—
You think they would have thought of something better by now.
I can hear the songbirds singing right now as I write this.
They have no idea I'm writing about them.
I have no idea they're singing about me.

The Matches in Our Matchbook

On the rack at the store there were magazines about women wearing clothes,
And there were magazines about women not wearing clothes,
And there were magazines about women wearing only a few clothes.
But there were no magazines at all about
Women who carry bugs outside rather than killing them.

I walked outside and the cloud formations reminded me of waiting in the car.
There's something to consider: life imitates *waiting in the car*.
When will they finally give us a magazine about waiting in the car?
When will they expose the head lice outbreak of Adlai Stevenson Junior High?
The goddamn microscopic animals, going from here to there,
With their microscopic pride, their microscopic grandeur—
It's about time that we notice the matches in our matchbook,
How civilized they really are, positioned the way they are,
So they all can see us, like spectators in a theater.

Progress

On the public transportation, I saw a middle-aged man
Rubbing petroleum jelly on his forehead.
For a second there, I confused him for an important curiosity,
But then the bus went through a five points intersection,
And suddenly he no longer seemed worthy of serious attention—
A nonsense figure rubbing medicinal ointment on his face.
So it was all just a false alarm but I'm not ashamed of my interest
In the man rubbing petroleum jelly on his forehead—

The bus was moving slowly down the street.
All of the passengers were making progress somehow.
Nobody riding the bus was a complete failure.
Don't ever say the bus didn't do anything for you.

This was in Milwaukee, and at one point,
The driver actually brought the bus to a complete stop
To allow for a squirrel to cross the street,
Which, truly, was an act of refined sophistication
Not available in the cultural centers.

The Poem Broke

I saw a plant in the window of an apartment above an apartment
Above a bar where the contractors go and it reminded me that
I've probably missed a good deal of poetry in my time.

The buildings aren't very tall in Milwaukee,
But you still die when you fall off of one.
They pulled the plug on my dying relative, and when they did,
It was part of an extension cord that included the woman in the next bed.
It's probably time to keep civilization out of reach of children.

My mother named me *Matt* after a Minneapolis travel agent
Who lost his sense of smell in a bizarre figure skating accident.
My mother joined the YMCA, which was absurd, because
My mother is not a Christian, she's not a man, and she's not young.

The flowerpot with the dirt and the plants and the flowers.
Your hand smells like onion from making dinner last night.
The poem broke because people handled it too often.

Constructive Criticism

I played trombone in this band in Milwaukee—
But my arms were really short,
So I couldn't hit any of the low notes on the trombone.

I was taking lessons from this guy downtown—
He was always trying to give me *constructive criticism*.
That's what he did—he gave constructive criticism
To trombone players with really short arms.

He was so dedicated, so patient, this guy downtown.
He was completely frank with me,
Absolutely candid about every possible matter—
Except for the length of my arms.
He would offer completely made-up, roundabout, very sweet,
Explanations as to why this or that horn part wasn't working.

He made it sound as though it were only a question of *gumption*.
He would never, ever, suggest that my arms were too short.

Walking Through Snow

A man told me that he reads my book while taking hot baths.
I tried to be friends with this guy but he was so loud and crazy,
Demanding that I eat organic strawberries in his car,
Attacking the commercial mayonnaise in my refrigerator.
He would tell me about polar bear documentaries he saw on TV.
He would show me plastic automotive debris he found behind the school.
He would demand that I come over to his house
In order to talk about how comedy was dead.
He'd apologize for actions that demanded no apology—
But then he'd actually try to impress me
With foolishness that *did* demand an apology.
He would call me up on the phone during blizzards
To ask if we could walk through the snow together—
But I like walking through the snow with crazy men, so I went.

Pocket Pool

It's obscene the way people put their fingers inside bowling balls.
It's obscene the way people play pocket pool
along central artery streets.
Is your mind in the gutter, or is your bowling ball in the gutter?
There's information to be gained from turning a sock inside out.
The electric doors will open up for everyone,
Even the illegitimate children.
It's adorable when people sit in cafes and write philosophical manifestos.
Go ahead and pour the banana batter
Into the muffin compartments and see if I care.
I saw a dog but I couldn't really see his face
Because his face was covered with dog.
You cannot see the sandwich in the man's stomach—
You must take his word for it.
The air conditioner above the door at the restaurant
Will drip on everyone, even the illegitimate children.
It's *obscene* the way people grow apples in New Zealand
And sell them for a profit in Indianapolis.
I don't care how much *volume* they're talking about—
They're losing money just to spite us.

One Encouraging Sign

The singer-songwriter singing outside his socio-economic station—
How does he pull it off? He *doesn't* pull it off—
He just doesn't *care*; and because he doesn't care, he pulls it off.
A useful organization would be something like Bad Taste Anonymous.
One encouraging sign is that people are sticking metal objects into toasters
With less and less regularity; I'm not sure of this, but I sense it somehow.

The zoo makes us sad but the arboretum makes us sadder.
The heroin addict vomiting into the mailbox seems inconsiderate at best.
Hanging a picture on a wall and liking it for a while and then not liking it.
Sometimes when you try to insert profundity into a poem,
It ends up looking like some guy tried to insert profundity into a poem.
I was in a foul mood until I saw Christians crammed into the extension van.
The sunlight will move slowly across the page as the airplane turns.
Who will inherit the task of recording butter's impact on bread?
Does it always have to be *me?*

Eclipse

I walked out of a bar in Milwaukee—
There was an eclipse in the night sky; I hardly even looked at it.
I bought a newspaper out of a machine; I walked slowly home.
Underneath the street lamps,
I read political arguments about Indian gaming rights.
Those arguments might not happen again for another 74 years.

Thank You

My body temperature was below normal; it was like 97.5—
It was like I was turning into a radio station,
Which was fine, because my radio had stopped working—
The batteries had died, beautifully, with dignity, in their sleep.

The morning paper seemed beyond me, but it was below me.
A piece of gunk fell out of my eye
And landed on an Associated Press photograph.
Russian business leaders with faces like water balloons—
Then a story about children hiding in a leaf pile who were hit by a van.

Then the photograph of the demonstrator outside the Federal building—
It was impossible to tell if he was shouting or yawning.

Thank you, Walt Whitman, for doing whatever it was you did
So that we don't have to write like they did before you came along.

American Notes (1842)

When Dickens got to Philadelphia,
He spent serious time with corn speculators.
He stayed at a boarding house where
They announced dinner with the clamor of a gong.
He saw blind people walking the streets,
Their eyes covered in green ribbon.
He drank tea with men of *varied attainments*.
This was back when oysters were
A lot more important than they are now.
Poorly educated men wearing boots
Would eat oysters in out-of-the-way bars.
Dickens always wanted to go to the courthouse,
The insane asylum and the prison;
Wherever he was, nothing would do but
The courthouse, the insane asylum and the prison.
Dickens would get completely flabbergasted whenever a prisoner
Would throw his clothing onto the floor.
His book has a whole paragraph about
Why it's bad for a prisoner to throw his clothing on the floor.
The prisoners in Pennsylvania
Would make paper hats and then wear them around.
The prisoners in Pennsylvania
Were allowed to keep rabbits if they wanted to.
When a lawyer would cross-examine a witness,
The lawyer would sit down at a table,
So he could write down the answers.
The doorknobs in Boston made a serious impression on Dickens;
There are actual sentences in his book

Devoted to the doorknobs in Boston.
Dickens asked his guide if he could watch
A group of Negroes eat lunch;
He wanted to tour a Negro's home with some cops.
Dickens found the frogs in Pennsylvania to be "almost incredible."
Dickens wrote that solitary confinement
"humanizes and refines" a woman's face.

Part Two

Where the Guy Used to Put the Milk

When the family would all get together in one room,
When the voices would all stir together,
You would hear this primitive confusion of authority—
Almost like the sound of your boss talking to your mom,
The sound of your wife talking to the cops,
The sound of your father's friend trying to remember
The falsehoods he read in the tabloid press.
The little box with the door on the side of the house
Where the guy used to put the milk.
The thick beer that everybody drank with a spoon—
The Norton Critical Edition of Your Mom.

You try to go to sleep in the basement of your father's new house.
You have a nightmare about being asleep and not being able to wake up.
You wake up in a strange bed in a foreign room—
Everything is black—
You have no idea where the lamp is; you flail your arms for it—
Looking for the lamp is actually worse than the nightmare.
You find the lamp; you turn it on.
It's a lamp you remember from your grandmother's house.
The little box with the door on the side of the house
Where the guy used to put the milk.
The box is painted shut.

Imaginary Lines

I was robbed by foolish teenagers who forgot to ask for the ideas
I was carrying around in my imagination.

When I was a boy, my brother would draw imaginary lines
On the bedroom floor, but then he would forget to tell me about them,
And I would walk across them—
You need to tell people about your imaginary lines—

The poem will have words falling
One behind the other like a Soviet bread line.
The transportation department will house enormous piles of rock salt
In buildings shaped like enormous piles of rock salt.

The traumatic event of one's childhood will involve
Bewilderment concerning the distribution of powdered sugar doughnuts.
It doesn't have to be anything more than that.
It doesn't have to involve the witnessing of the ironworker's bloated corpse
Following the unforeseen crane accident in the hard hat zone.
No, no—we're talking about comprehensive humiliation
Brought on by *bewilderment* relating to powdered sugar doughnuts.

The mother rabbit will get run over by the stationwagon in the street.
The baby rabbits will get pecked to death by crows—
The comfortable childhood of the baby crows will go unreported.

The Child

The child will prefer the nickel to the dime
Because the nickel has greater substance.
I still have a certain respect for that sort of reasoning.
The iron dog by the door with the blade running along its backbone
Where the child will scrape off the muddy shoes.
The ring of synthetic fur around the hood of one's coat.

There was a mathematics teacher at my school
Who would walk the halls wearing a paisley ascot tie—
But I was never good enough at math to be in his class.
But it was clear to me, even then,
That the children who *were* good enough to be in his class
Were not sufficiently in awe of his paisley ascot tie.

Back During the Twentieth Century

When I was a boy I colored my entire forearm
Yellow with fluorescent marking pen and then
I told my parents that I had yellow fever.
I wanted to make myself look sick so that
I could stay home from school.

This was back during the Twentieth Century when
Everybody had magic markers in their dining room drawers.
But nobody was *satisfied* with that—
They wanted supernatural pencils
That wrote with the grease of synthetic cuttlefish.

Bad Potato Scholarship

This boy I went to grade school with
Was so brilliant that he could fold paper *airports*.
He lived down by the tennis facility where the streets got all curvy.
His mother would make this stuff called *ukulele bread*,
Which was bread with little bits of ukulele in it.
We would eat that bread, and then we would play dead in his backyard.
We understood, even as children, that playing dead
Was more fun than playing backgammon.
His father was a retired potato scholar at the university.
He was so famous for his potato scholarship
That he could get away with writing
Comparatively bad potato scholarship
And still have it published in the leading journals.
All of the younger potato scholars were
Jealous of him and thought he was a lazy hack.
I always wanted to be a fly on a wall in that boy's home—
But a fly with at least a basic understanding of commercial agriculture.

This

I'm delighted when my dreams do not come true
Because my dreams typically involve myself,
Naked, being torn apart by wild cats in the town square,
In plain view of cynical adults who feel no remorse
At overcharging for lemon–lime soft drinks.

Having your back against the wall, I think,
Is actually more comfortable than facing the wall.
To say that the suspense is killing you is to miss the point.
The suspense is not killing you; the *narrative* is killing you.
The suspension of disbelief is killing you.

Static Electricity

Remember static electricity?
Whatever happened to static electricity?
That sure seemed to come up more when we were younger.
People would rub balloons against their heads,
And then stick the balloons to walls;
People would make examples out of the balloons they stuck to walls.
The suggestion was that they were illustrating a principle,
Something that would have future applications.
But there *were* no other applications—
It was just people rubbing balloons against their heads
And sticking the balloons to walls, and saying *static electricity*.

Nonsense

His grandmother, for example, was pathologically no-nonsense.
He was aware, then, that his nonsense was
Built on the backs of a lot of other people's no-nonsense.
He would have apologized to everyone for his nonsense,
But he understood how little sense it made to apologize for nonsense.

It was difficult enough for him to drive a motor vehicle.
Driving was a function where nonsense was not permitted.
When the traffic light turns green, you absolutely must go,
Whether or not it is the truly beautiful thing to do.
He was the first generation in his family to have a problem with this.

My Pen

I had no idea that I would write about Hungarian Goulash today.
It just came right out of my pen—
Hungarian Goulash just came right out of my pen today.
It might just as easily have come out of your pen, Hungarian Goulash,
But it came out of my pen instead.
And then I went and had the whole thing copyrighted,
So now it would be against the law for Hungarian Goulash
To come out of your pen in even a similar kind of way.
It's not easy to become a man like me.
I made the right kind of *choices* in my life
So that Hungarian Goulash could
Come out of my pen when I needed it to.
I *positioned myself* to benefit from
Hungarian Goulash coming out of my pen.

The Pants in This City

There are more pants in this city than there are people.

There are more *pockets* than there are pants.

There are pennies in the pockets of people's pants in this city.

There are pencils behind people's ears, occasionally.

There are isolated pockets

Of people wearing pants with pockets in this city.

There are puny little pictures of people

On the pennies in the pockets of people's pants in this city.

There are pieces of paper in the pockets of people's pants.

There are confirmation notices in the pockets of people's pants.

There are pencils behind the people's *ears* sometimes.

There are puppies with microchips implanted in their foreheads.

Thank God for that. Thank God we'll never lose that puppy again!

There are lost puppy notification fliers

Posted in the park with Polaroid snapshots.

There are *problems* with the lost puppy Polaroids in the park.

There are serious problems with *creative control* on lost puppy fliers.

I would like to see *photo credits*

On lost puppy notification fliers in the park.

The *actual person* who took the Polaroid,

I would like to see his or her name, in small lettering,

Alongside the picture of the lost puppy in the park.

Maybe

I thought that this girl didn't like me,
Which wasn't actually true,
But by the time I found out that she liked me,
She didn't really like me anymore.
But it wasn't as though she *disliked* me; it wasn't quite like that.
She was somewhere between like and dislike,
At least from what people were telling me.
Really, I think that she liked me,
But it was a like that was diminishing gradually,
And before she could reach any kind of dislike for me,
I think she just flat out stopped thinking about me,
Which, probably, is worse than dislike, when you think of it,
But I've been wrong before.

Her

Her neck looked like part of a bottle.
Her eyes looked like hurricanes.
Her ears looked like corn.
Her mouth looked like the beginning of a river.
Her elbows looked like dried macaroni product.
Her heart looked like the inside of an artichoke.
Her head really looked like a cauliflower.

Summary of Pittsburgh

I read this summary of Pittsburgh in six paragraphs one time.
I was over at a girl's house
And she had all these brochures that were about Pittsburgh.
She wanted to relocate out to the Pittsburgh area
So she was filling out applications to schools in Pittsburgh.
So she had all this literature and one of the brochures
Was talking up the various cultural aspects of Pittsburgh—
Trying to lure you to Pittsburgh with cultural aspects.
But this one brochure I'm talking about had
A summary of Pittsburgh in six paragraphs.
The first paragraph started off
With general declarations about Pittsburgh,
Followed by successive paragraphs
That reinforced ideas forecasted in the first paragraph.
The final paragraph ended up wrapping the whole thing up—
Recapping ideas established throughout the summary of Pittsburgh—
So it was like this conventionally organized
Summary of Pittsburgh in six paragraphs.
It was as though Pittsburgh had all its shit together
In this brochure I found at this girl's house.

Tequila

I got very drunk on tequila one time
When I was staying on a chicken farm in California,
And I had to go outside and vomit in the middle of the night.
I walked out to where the cars were parked and I vomited near a tree.
After that I went back inside and tried to get some sleep.
But a while later I felt like I had to vomit again.
I went back out to the same tree by where the cars were parked,
But when I got there I noticed that my vomit from before was gone.
I remember thinking that was strange,
But I was very sick and so I didn't dwell on it too much.
I just vomited again and went back inside and I tried to go to sleep.
A little while later I felt like I had to vomit again,
So I walked back outside and *again* my vomit was gone.
My vomit was just gone—
My vomit kept disappearing somehow.
I really started to think I was losing my mind at that point.
Eventually, I don't know, I just passed out somehow.
In the morning, though, everything became very clear.
I woke up and I walked outside and I sat in a folding chair.
The chickens were hurrying over toward me;
They circled around me with a kind of needy excitement.

Room for Cream
For Carl Bogner

The worker at the coffee shop asks you if you need room for cream.
You can't really isolate the moment when this began happening—
Nineteen ninety-two, A.D., perhaps.
Somewhere along the way, for whatever reason,
You not only wanted room for cream,
You wanted to be asked whether you needed room for cream.
Did your father need room for cream?
Are you the first generation in your family to need room for cream?
Can you remember what things were like
Before you needed room for cream?
Was your character somehow stronger?
Were you able to just tough things out?
Did you simply drink some off the top before adding cream?
I'm thinking that that's what you did—
I'm thinking that maybe you did *without* room for cream,
I'm thinking that you probably made do
With *nowhere near enough* room for cream.

Part Three

Memoir

When the drunk man tells you about his day,
He's speaking from autobiography.
When the four disappointing old men
Attempt to impress the one disappointing young woman,
Frequently, they're speaking from autobiography.
Who knew that it was possible to make a mockery of a puppet show?
Oftentimes a man is not intelligent enough to know
That his intelligence has just been insulted—
When this happens, the man finds himself neither intelligent nor insulted,
Which, in a way, is brilliant and infuriating.
Only a schizophrenic man will actually call a radio station with a request.
When I was a boy, there were people who would tell jokes about
Countries that performed poorly during the Second World War.
The theme still had a certain resonance somehow.
The jokes would involve representatives of
Different nationalities parachuting out of an airplane—
The last person to fall to the ground revealed the point of the story.
Will artificial intelligence
Ever advance to the point of appreciating an insult?
Just listen to the man tell you about the things he saw on television—
Just listen to him; he's speaking from autobiography.

The Waitresses

The waitresses
At the restaurant
Have to keep reminding
The schizophrenic man
That if he keeps acting
Like a schizophrenic man
They'll have to ask him to leave the restaurant.
But he keeps *forgetting* that he's a schizophrenic man,
So they have to keep *reminding* him.

Shipwreck

Ships got into wrecks often enough
That it made sense to compound the words together.
The word itself was the real unforeseen accident—*shipwreck*.
It happened without warning.
Nobody was prepared for the *word* shipwreck.
Doors existed independently of knobs for a period of time
Until we put knobs onto doors and called them doorknobs.
Look at that worm over there, the one inside the man's intestine!
That worm looks a like a whip!
Let's call that worm a *whipworm*.
Thank god for the erratic whimsicality of intestinal worm names!
Poetry, you know, is the only forum we have
For showing our gratitude for intestinal worm names.
How about putting soap into boxes for a sustained period of time
Until it finally makes sense to call those boxes soapboxes—
How about doing that—
Look at that intestinal worm over there!
It sure looks like a whip—
Let's call that worm a *whipworm*.

Visualize the Governor

It's absurd the way your mind's eye can visualize the governor.
You go through your days,
You're barely even conscious of the governor at all,
But then suddenly the subject turns to the governor,
And then there's a need to visualize the governor,
And then there he is, there's the governor, in your mind's eye—
He's like a composite of old newspaper photographs,
Photographs of the governor you carry around in your imagination—
His upper body mostly, the upper body of the governor,
His face and his dark suit and his dark tie.
It's just weird to me that you can visualize
The governor on command like that.
Even when he's no longer the governor,
When he's only the *former* governor,
When he's nothing more than a prominent retired man,
You still have the ability to visualize the governor.

Goat Transactions

Writing began, of course, as a scheme to better recall the past.
People were having serious problems remembering their memories.
They kept forgetting their memories, or misremembering their memories.
It was time for ideas to move away from an ephemeral arrangement
And into a more concrete arrangement.
Ideas needed to become *documents*—
Exactly the design we're moving away from now.

Writing began, you know, as a way of recording goat transactions.
It became very critical that goat transactions be remembered properly.
With goat transactions, civilization finally had something
That it could no longer afford to forget.
Writing, you could say, was the result of
An effort to *reform* goat transactions.
Writing became necessary, probably, only in response to
Widespread corruption in goat transactions.

These People

He ran in circles of wool buyers and wool sellers and wool middlemen.
He actually knew people who were wool middlemen.
And then he also knew these other people,
Who were not wool middlemen at all, but who made it their business
To offer unsolicited advice to people who were wool middlemen—
They were essentially like *armchair* wool middlemen.
This was his world; these were his people; he understood these people.
He understood what became of the wool middlemen.
He understood what became of the adult children of wool middlemen.
He understood what became of the adult children of *armchair* wool middlemen.

His Problem

This was his problem:
His imagination would sometimes hold beautiful things,
But he was not able to remove those beautiful things
Without them becoming ugly things.
Beauty was not able to survive
The journey from his mind to the outside world;
He was not able to safeguard beauty from ugliness.
He did not understand, somehow,
That beauty was a foreign language that needed to be translated.
Like someone with bad taste,
He would often confuse beauty for ugliness;
Or, like someone with bad taste,
He would encounter ugliness and confuse it for beauty.
He would record ugly thoughts into his notebook, for example,
And then he would fail to notice that they were ugly thoughts,
He would fail to dispose of them immediately.
Instead, like a fool, he would bring them into a public forum.
There were, I remember, a few occasions
Where he was able to circumvent these obstacles,
Where he did manage to create truly beautiful works.
But whenever this would happen,
He would always insist on making the pieces "better"
At which point he would unknowingly surround them with ugliness,
Thus making the beauty invisible.
That, really, was his problem:
He had no control over his ability to make beauty invisible.

Grant's Tomb

I was standing outside Grant's Tomb on a very hot day.
There were fashion models doing a photo shoot in front of Grant's Tomb.
But they were not striking models; they were like JC Penney mom models.
And the fashion people weren't even concerned with Grant's Tomb;
They just wanted the models up against Neoclassical columns.
And the cellphone reception is really bad around Grant's Tomb.
I wanted to cancel my service, citing poor reception around Grant's Tomb.
But what I'm saying is, it was so damn hot outside that
I ordered a chicken sandwich, denied it, and walked away.
There was a street vendor there, up by Grant's Tomb,
And I ordered a chicken sandwich, but it was so damn hot that day
That I just ordered it and stood there in the heat and forgot that I ordered it.
And then the vendor asked me if I wanted onions on that—
I just looked at him and said, "I never ordered any chicken sandwich."
And I just walked away up the street.
That's what happened to me up by Grant's Tomb,
I ordered a chicken sandwich, denied it, and walked away.

An Obligation

Just look at the Seeing Eye dog!
So trustworthy, the Seeing Eye dog!
Never a moment's doubt about the Seeing Eye dog!
Yet surely the Seeing Eye dog could be corrupted by, say, succulent meats.
Surely the introduction of, say, delicious sausage,
At the exact right moment, could distract the dog
Just as his master is moving toward oncoming traffic.
I read somewhere that Seeing Eye dog is actually a registered trademark—
I suppose the question then becomes:
What if the Seeing Eye dog had an obligation to its stockholders?

According to the Officer

My wife was walking
Home from work one day
When a lewd man wearing
An Army surplus greatcoat
Exposed himself to her.
My wife made her way home safely
And then phoned the police who sent over an officer.
Apparently, according to the officer,
The police had already received complaints
About the man in the greatcoat.
But, according to the officer,
In most cases, the victims
Tended to be younger women.
So, essentially, my wife got flashed
And the cops came over
And told her she looked old.

A Girl in Milwaukee and a Girl in Brooklyn

My wife is talking on the phone in Milwaukee
To her girlfriend in Brooklyn.
But, in the middle of all that, my wife has to go pee.
And it turns out that the girl in Brooklyn,
At the very same time, also has to go pee.
So they discuss this for a moment,
And they're both very intelligent people.
They decide to set their phones down and go to the bathroom
(This was back when people set their phones down).
So they do this, and now we have a live telephone line open
Between Milwaukee and Brooklyn
With no one speaking through it for about two minutes as
A girl in Milwaukee and a girl in Brooklyn go to the bathroom.

Part Four

Worse Than Fruit Bats

The road to hell is paved with poorly worded epigrams.
The dogs will run upstairs as though they understand why.
You will meet a new friend, and you will go over to his house,
And you will realize that you've turned around in his driveway before.
The way people's belts generally go through their belt loops.
The forks and spoons will look bigger standing in the glass of water—
Indeed, we've already established that.
The leaves will forget to fall off the trees in the wintertime,
And they will become shriveled like fruit bats, or worse than fruit bats.
You will get mad when the smoke alarm goes off
And you're drunk and making grilled cheese sandwiches.
But the smoke alarm is *right*—
You *are* drunk and making grilled cheese sandwiches.

This River

We're all in the same boat but the boat is awful,
And the conversation is bad and long and difficult.
An unfinished cylinder is a cylinder that's not quite a cylinder.
A girl from outside Chicago will say she's from Chicago.
The drunken plans to get together for breakfast tomorrow.
The medical doctor who finds himself rooting for
Someone's pancreas to become inflamed.

The undergraduates will say Socrates in such a way
That it sounds like they're saying *soccer cheese*.
Who knows, maybe *they are* saying soccer cheese.
What I do know is the name of this river.
But this river does not know my name.
I'm hoping, someday, to meet a river
That can reciprocate this basic courtesy.

Contingency Plan

I'm sitting across from a man whose body is falling apart.
But he's lost in thought right now;
He's off somewhere in a moment of thought.
He's not even aware, really, that his body's falling apart.
You almost want to tell him that his body's falling apart.
You wonder if he has *a contingency plan*
For when his body really starts to fall apart.
Now he's laughing to himself;
He couldn't care less that his body's falling apart.
He's sitting in the restaurant by the window near the chrome entranceway.
He has a steaming cup of coffee, the sky is blue outside behind him.
Wait a minute—he just wiped something off of his face.
He's clearly thinking about something else right now.

Oxford

The people at the restaurant—look at them.
They look like really intelligent monkeys.
Look at them closely, they really do.
Brilliant monkeys—monkeys that went to Oxford, for crying out loud.
Just watch the man drink his lemonade.
He looks like a monkey of extreme refinement.
No, no—I didn't expect a monkey of this quality.

A More Refined Slant

Everyone had to agree
That he was so much more fun when
His lungs weren't filling up with mucus.

He said that his education did nothing for him except
Cause him to look at the floor with a more refined slant,
Which, he conceded, was not nothing.

His onion soup was so easy to make
That his friends lost all respect for him.

His mother thought the parking meters had destroyed downtown.
But really it was civilization that had destroyed downtown.
Then his car wouldn't run because the engine died, with dignity,
Surrounded by its friends, in a warm garage.

He wasn't wearing his glasses one day and he
Thought he saw a fur hat drinking out of a bowl in the kitchen,
But it was really just *his cat* drinking out of a bowl in the kitchen.

Then his lungs started filling up with mucus some more
And then he died, but in a better place, a place where
People donated their bodies to the liberal arts.

The Grave

A poet that I admire
Is buried in one of those very old cemeteries
Where the stone markers are faded
And fallen and overgrown with moss and all that.
The poet's grave is unmarked.

I found an eccentric old man
Who was a kind of weird *cemetery extremist*.
I was introduced to him through the historical society,
And he explained to me how to find the poet's grave.
He gave me detailed instructions that involved references
To specific trees in the cemetery.

I went there and I walked around and I found the stone marker
And I stood there and I looked at it for about fifteen minutes.
The cars were going by on the highway and they sounded funny.
The cars on the highway will sound different
When you're looking at a grave.
I actually prefer the way the cars sound
When you're *not* looking at a grave.

Then some months went by
And again I saw the weird old cemetery extremist.
I told him about my experience at the graveyard
And his face collapsed immediately into disappointment.
I had completely mishandled his directions.
The poet's grave was near where I was, he said,
But it was not the grave I admired.

No Idea

They landed a camera on Mars today,
Which was fine and everything,
But I was still working on Noel Coward.
I wasn't *through* yet with Noel Coward.
I was still trying to figure out what the deal was with Noel Coward,
And then they went and put a camera up on Mars,
Which was fine and everything, but when they do something like that,
I've found, it has a way of *presupposing*
That we're all done with Noel Coward,
That we're somehow ready to move past Noel Coward.

Around that same time I talked to a man
Who did not know that potatoes grew underground.
He was very excited about the camera they put up on Mars.
He had no idea that potatoes grew underground.

Two Police Officers

You know how at the library
They have those dictionaries
Sitting on pedestals or whatever?
You know what I'm talking about.
Well, I was walking through the library,
Up on the third floor, and I saw two police officers
Standing over this dictionary.
Two police officers, fully armed, standing over a dictionary.
Never before had I even *associated*
A police officer with a dictionary—ever.
I had never once imagined the idea
Of an on-duty, uniformed police officer
Looking Something Up in the Dictionary.
But now I was watching *two* police officers
Looking Something Up in the Dictionary, *together*.
The vision was so striking that I seriously questioned
Whether the dictionary was somehow involved in a crime scene.
But no, this was far more sensational than that;
This was two police officers Looking Something Up in the Dictionary.

Not Convinced

What's wrong with *tomorrow?*
Tomorrow will *also* be the first day of the rest of your life.
Today is the last holiday before the first day of the rest of your life.
Let's take these caterpillar cocoons
And make scarves and neckties out of them—
Any fool can see that that's more impressive than the Internet.

Wait—I thought the president said we would
Prevail against having to wake up in the morning.
I thought that every chair could open up like a piano bench,
If only we had the courage.

The people who fix our broken things will take our money,
And they will buy different things that will break—
Things that *they* would like to see break.
Venetian blinds that go up and down and up and down and then break.

The television will be talking to itself in the next room.
America needs to resolve its complicated relationship with the bearded man!
The bearded man at work! The bearded man at home!
The bearded man *in general!*
The voice will be the voice of the failed acting workshop student—
His dreams giving way to apple cinnamon flavored cream cheese commercials.

I'm not completely convinced that taking deep breaths
Will have any noticeable impact on this situation.

Hit Parade

Have you ever knocked someone down,
Stepped in their face, and slandered their name all over the place?
Have you ever been in a situation where an old-fashioned love song
Was coming down in three-part harmony?
Have you ever laid tracks for troubadours who got
Killed before they reached Bombay?
Have you reached the point where something was
Flowing through the jasmine of your mind?
Have you ever known someone whose
Independence seemed to vanish in the haze?
Have you ever noticed that the nation was
Turning its lonely eyes to Joe DiMaggio?
Have you ever met a store-bought woman
Who made you sing like a guitar humming?
Have you ever just for a moment thought—
Ooh, ooh, child, things are gonna get brighter?
Have you ever been so mad about saffron
That saffron was actually mad about you?

The Noises

Surely I'll die not understanding the noises my furnace makes.
It's probably easier, I'm thinking,
Just to *accept* the noises my furnace makes.

The payphone will give your coin back out of simple fairness.
I've met a few bad telephones,
But most of them are decent and trustworthy.
You realize, over time, that an elderberry tree
Is a tree that bears elderberries.

O to be young and in love and buying ant poison at a hardware store—
Some people will climb aluminum staircases during electrical storms
To save three and one half dollars on one dozen two-ply paper towels.

Some people will walk into a store
And buy morally superior dishwashing liquid.
They will buy dishwashing liquid whose biodegradability
Far exceeds legislative requirements.
They will reflect on this matter later, and they will become sentimental
About the reactionary dishwashing soap they left at home.

The Point

It got to the point where *you could* buy time—
You could buy time at the hardware store—
They sold the stuff in paint cans, where the lid would pry off,
And 45 minutes would spill out.
It got to the point where,
Not only could you buy happiness,
You could buy happiness in *squeeze bottles*.
It got to the point where you *could* make a silk purse out of a sow's ear.

The Corn Inspector

Well dog my cats, here comes the corn inspector!
Somebody has to be the corn inspector; we all know that—
Somebody *must* be the corn inspector; there's really no way around it.
But eventually the corn company will come along,
And they will decide to enforce random drug testing.
It will become a matter of *inspecting* the corn inspector—
Well dog my cats, they're inspecting the corn inspector!

Oblong Strongboxes

We trust the men wearing the official hats
They bought at the uniform supply store.
We trust the public school teacher
With the deformed hands and the checkered shirt.

Beauty is always sentimental when you come right down to it—
Except for the fashion models
With the sunglasses, who look like terrible insects.

Someday you'll grow old
And you'll put periods at the ends of your sentences.
You'll take your shoes off and leave them in the hallway.
Someday you'll look up *green* or *blue* in a standard dictionary—
You'll look them up for the laughs you can get.

You like the way they store the dead people underground—
The oblong strongboxes, the satin stretched over the upholstery foam.
You like that approach; you're all for that approach.
You were mad, I remember, when they covered your friend
With newspapers and packing peanuts.

The Man Across the Street

He was on the vanguard of belligerent simplicity—
Angry at something downstairs, angry at something downtown,
Talking to the boxes stacked up in his garage.
He would bully people into buying his old bus transfers.
He would call the police when the church bells disturbed the peace.

Whenever there was a winter storm,
And there were serious snowdrifts his backyard,
He would open up his basement windows,
And he would shovel the snow through his basement windows
And onto his basement floor, where, presumably,
It would become water, or something, and run down his basement drain.
He was the only man on the block who would do this.
The rest of us would always *fumble* the opportunity.

Wait, look—there's the man
Across the street who inspired me yesterday.
His value has clearly diminished overnight.
He's essentially worthless now.
The planet went around once
And the man across the street became worthless.
Thanks for going around once, you no-account planet.

The Center of the Earth

We use the center of the Earth everyday without even thinking about it.
The mailman couldn't be the mailman without the center of the Earth.
When the radio falls into the bathtub,
It's only falling toward the center of the Earth.
It *means well*, the radio, when it falls into the bathtub.

It's probably darker than the inside of a cow at the center of the Earth.
I actually saw the inside of a cow one time at a state fair.
They had a live cow there, and they had affixed a plastic window
To the side of its body, so that you could look in there,
And you could see the inside of a cow—
But it was no longer darker than the inside of a cow in there,
Because they had affixed that window,
Which was flooding a lot of light inside the cow,
Which was obscuring the reality of the cow, the poetry of the cow.

Nostalgia

I liked it back when shoe salesmen pretended to care.
There was comfort in the false kindness of shoe salesmen.
Civilization was *preferable* when shoe salesmen pretended to care.
Thanks for pretending to care!
Look at me, I'm nostalgic for insincere shoe salesmen!

The End of the World

We learned through experience how unimportant our experience was.
The English language was the only language where spelling god
Backward amounted to something whimsical and satisfying.
It's no longer possible, really, to imagine a world where
Dangerous thugs spoke seriously of *knuckle sandwiches*.
The worst bully in my school
Was the son of the only honest mechanic in town.
Yet they both grew into remote old men who abused book club offers—
They were completely determined, both of them,
To abuse the book club before the book club could abuse them.
The end of the world will come in monthly installments.
The end of the world will be bothersome
Yet tolerable, like a drink that smells funny.
My friend was completely lost on a mountain in Peru.
Nevertheless, he still bothered to make
A photograph of himself preparing scrambled eggs.
The end of the world will be exactly like that.

Parallel Parking

A man was trying to parallel park his car in the snow.
He had no idea that a poet
Was watching him through a plate glass window.
It turned out that the poet in the window
Benefited from the man in the car
Considerably more than the man in the car
Benefited from the poet in the window.

Yet futility keeps teaching you the same thing over and over again.
I gather that people want to move past futility,
Into a period of post futility, but of course they're just being silly;
I'll put my money on futility.
A fruit fly landed on my shirt
And I reached for him and he was dead.

To my children, rock and roll will sound
Like funny harpsichord music.
Rock and roll died, you know,
Before anyone wrote a song about aluminum foil.
Van Gogh was an insane man capable of self-mutilation and yet
His paintings went on to become thank you notes for grandmothers.
The wrong people will understand
The right way to make the wrong decisions.
The copywriters will compose persuasive love poetry saying that
Your invisible tape isn't your father's invisible tape.

Is there anything else to say about cucumber sandwiches?
Will there always be something else to say

About cucumber sandwiches?
Will we forget what we said about cucumber sandwiches
And need to say it again?
Are we in denial that we've run out of things to say
About cucumber sandwiches?

About the Author

Matt Cook appeared in the five-part PBS series, *The United States of Poetry*, produced by Washington Square Films. His poem 'James Joyce' was aired on National Public Radio's *Fresh Air with Terry Gross* during a broadcast about spoken word in 1996. He also wrote and performed the original poem 'Picabo Street' for a nationally televised commercial for Nike during the 1998 Winter Olympics. It was chosen by *Adweek* magazine as one of the Best Creative Spots of February 1998. Several poems from his first book, *In the Small of My Backyard*, have been read by Garrison Keillor on NPR's *Writers Almanac*. Matt Cook lives in Milwaukee. This is his second book.

Manic D Press Poetry Books

Some Angels Wear Black. Eli Coppola. $13.95

Madness and Retribution. Juliette Torrez. $13.95

The Beautiful. Michelle Tea. $13.95

The Splinter Factory. Jeffrey McDaniel. $13.95

The Forgiveness Parade. Jeffrey McDaniel. $11.95

Alibi School. Jeffrey McDaniel. $11.95

Walking Barefoot in the Glassblowers Museum. Ellyn Maybe. $13.95

In the Small of My Backyard. Matt Cook. $13.95

Monster Fashion. Jarret Keene. $13.95

Harmless Medicine. Justin Chin. $13.95

Bite Hard. Justin Chin. $13.95

Poetry Slam: the competitive art of performance poetry. G. Glazner, ed. $15

Concrete Dreams: Manic D Press Early Works, Jennifer Joseph, ed., $15

Cottonmouth Kisses. Clint Catalyst. $12.95

Sorry We're Close. J. Tarin Towers. $11.95

Growing Up Free In America. Bruce Jackson. $11.95

Monkey Girl. Beth Lisick. $11.95

Hell Soup: the collected writings of Sparrow 13 LaughingWand. $8.95

King of the Roadkills. Bucky Sinister. $9.95

Revival: Spoken Word from Lollapalooza 94. Torrez et al., eds. $12.95

Signs of Life: channel-surfing through '90s culture. Joseph, ed. $12.95

Beyond Definition. Blackman & Healey, eds. $10.95

The Verdict Is In. edited by Kathi Georges & Jennifer Joseph. $9.95

The Back of a Spoon. Jack Hirschman. $7

Baroque Outhouse/Decapitated Head of a Dog. Randolph Nae. $7

Greatest Hits. edited by Jennifer Joseph. $7

Lizards Again. David Jewell. $7

The Future Isn't What It Used To Be. Jennifer Joseph. $7

Please add $4 to all orders for postage and handling.
Manic D Press, Inc. • Box 410804 • San Francisco CA 94141 USA
info@manicdpress.com   www.manicdpress.com